THANK A FARMER

WRITTEN BY
ANDREA KIRCHOFF

Thank a Farmer
Copyright © 2021 by Andrea Kirchoff

All rights reserved. No part of this publication may be reproduced, distributed, or transmitted in any form or by any means, including photocopying, recording, or other electronic or mechanical methods, without the prior written permission of the author, except in the case of brief quotations embodied in critical reviews and certain other non-commercial uses permitted by copyright law.

Tellwell Talent
www.tellwell.ca

ISBN
978-0-2288-5604-7 (Hardcover)
978-0-2288-5603-0 (Paperback)

For my son Graham

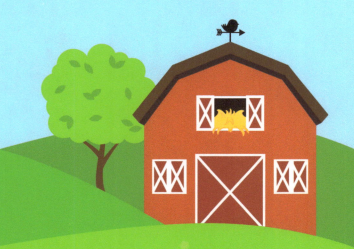

"Okay, Graham, let's see what's on our grocery list."

"Wow, mom, the grocery store grows a lot of food."

"Well, Graham, the grocery store didn't grow our food. The farmers did. The grocery store buys from the farmers and sells it to us. This way, we can buy all our yummy food in one place."

"Milk is first on our list, Graham."

"Well, where does our milk come from, mom?"

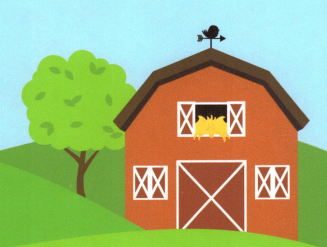

"Milk comes from cows on a dairy farm. On average, cows are fed about one hundred pounds of food per day and drink around thirty-five gallons of water—that's as much as us eating a hundred boxes of cereal per day! Cows get milked two to three times every day, producing around eight to nine gallons of milk. After the cows are milked, the creamy-white milk is cooled in tanks until a tanker comes to pick it up. Then the tanker takes it to a processing plant where the milk is pasteurized. The word pasteurized means that milk is heated to a temperature that kills harmful germs and then is cooled before it gets bottled and delivered to the grocery store. Let's thank a farmer so that kids like you can enjoy fresh, creamy milk every day."

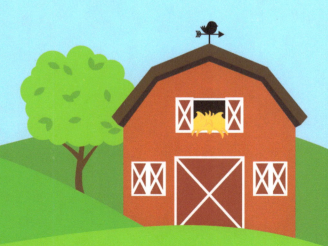

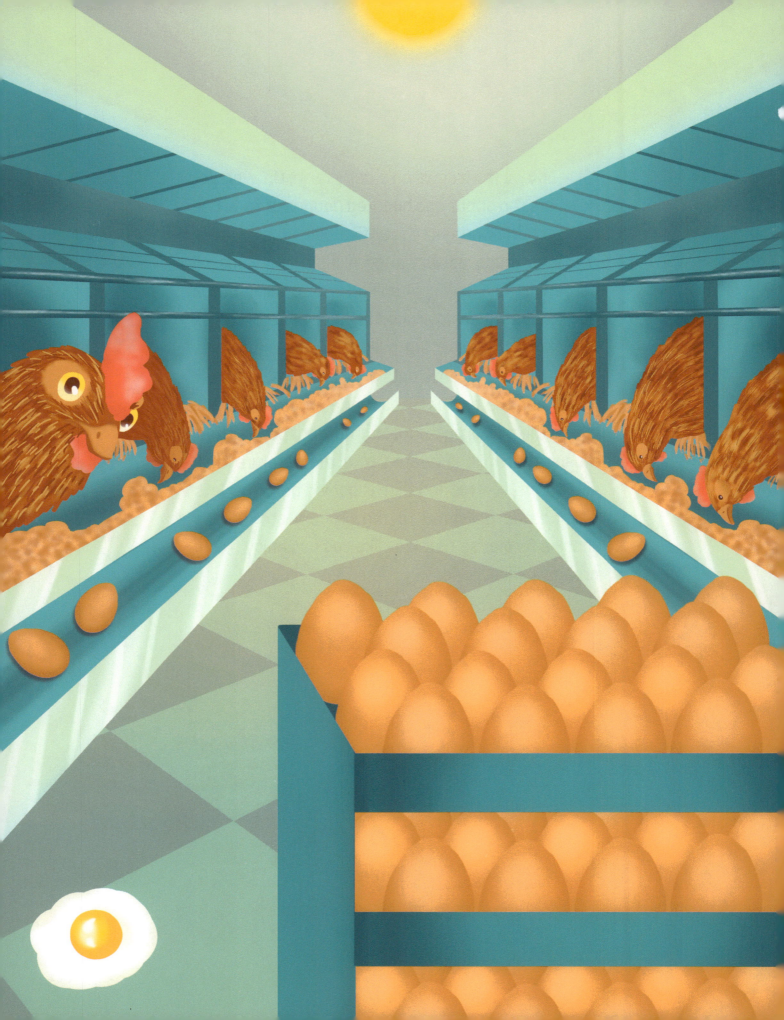

"Eggs are next."

"So, where do eggs come from, mom?"

"Hens lay around one egg per day. Have you ever seen different colored eggs? This depends on the breed of the hen and the color of feathers over the hen's ears. Hens take dust baths to keep themselves clean–no bubble baths for these girls. Hens lay their eggs in nesting boxes with a conveyor belt underneath. The conveyor belt collects the eggs, and they are taken into the packing house. The eggs are then sorted and packed for shipping to the grocery store. Let's thank a farmer so that kids like you can enjoy sunny side up or scrambled eggs for breakfast."

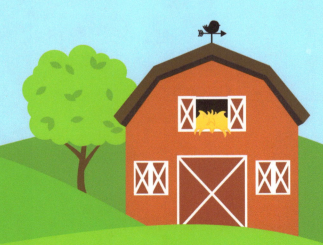

"Almonds are next on our list."

"How are almonds grown, mom?"

"Did you know almonds are grown on trees? When almonds are ready for harvest in late August, the shaker machine shakes each tree for three to four seconds so that the almonds fall off the tree. A sweeper then sweeps the nuts into the center of each row. Next, the tractor goes through each row and picks up the nuts. The nuts then get dumped into a loader so that they can travel up an elevator into a truck and get taken to the huller. Once at the huller, they go through a sifter to separate the twigs and stones from the nuts. Then they go through a cracking machine that separates the hull from the nut. The hull cracks, and the almonds come out. They then get sent to another sifter that separates the almonds from the bits of the hull. The hulls are saved for feed for cows or sent for processing for almond oil. The almonds are sent to large bins and stored until they are ready to ship to the grocery store. Let's thank a farmer so that kids like you can enjoy a healthy snack of almonds in your trail mix."

"Tomatoes are next on our grocery list."

"How are tomatoes grown, mom?"

"In the spring, tomato seeds can be planted in transplant trays for super-strong plants to grow before they are planted in the field. Once the transplants are ready, the trays are taken to the field, where a machine called a transplanter plants them in the ground. The transplants get pulled out of each tray and are dropped into a rotating cup on the transplanter. The transplants go down a shoot and get pushed into the ground. As the tomatoes grow, they get tied up to prevent breakage because the fruit gets so heavy that it could break the plant vines. The transplants use the sun and rain to help them grow red, round fruit. When the tomatoes are ready for harvest, they are picked, sorted, cleaned, and boxed for the grocery store. Let's thank a farmer so that kids like you can enjoy tasty tomatoes on your cheeseburgers."

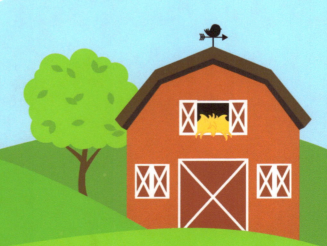

"Potatoes are next on our grocery list."

"How are potatoes grown, mom?"

"Farmer's plant small potatoes underground in the spring. After some time, potato roots shoot out and grow green plants above the ground, but the potatoes we eat, grow underground–this is called a root crop. When the potatoes are ready, the green plant above the ground dies. Harvesting starts with potato harvesters, which are machines that dig under the earth and pull out the potatoes. The potatoes are carried on a conveyor that drops them into the trailers. The potatoes are then taken to the packing house, where they are sent to another conveyor to be washed, sorted, and packed, then shipped to the grocery store. Let's thank a farmer so that kids like you can enjoy crispy French fries."

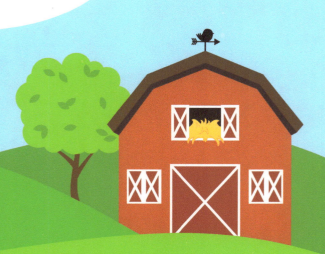

"Pineapple is next on our grocery list."

"How are pineapples grown, mom?"

"Pineapples grow from the center of a sword-like leafy plant. This fruit takes a very long time to grow. From planting to flowering, it takes a little over two years. Whoa! From there, it takes six months for the sweet, juicy yellow fruit to be ready for harvest. The farmer checks the sugar content and decides if the pineapple is ready to be picked. Pineapples are plucked by hand and put onto a conveyor, where they are stacked upside down into a trailer. They can bruise easily, so packing them upside down into the container helps cushion them for the ride. When the container is full, it is taken to the packing house to be packed and shipped to the grocery store. Let's thank a farmer so that kids like you can enjoy a sweet, juicy pineapple in your fruit salad."

"Honey is last on our grocery list."

"Where does honey come from, mom?"

"Bees make honey, and beekeepers harvest the extra honey from the beehive that the bees don't need to survive the winter. The beekeeper builds a beehive that holds frames filled with wax in which the bees store their honey. Bees need nectar to make honey, which comes from flowers. Honey bees go from flower to flower to collect nectar. A bee travels to nearly a thousand flowers to fill its stomach full of nectar. Bees have two stomachs, but only one holds the nectar. Once the bee has a full load of nectar in its tummy, it travels back to the hive to drop it off. Bees have an enzyme in their stomach that helps thicken the nectar to make the sticky honey you love so much. Once it's thick enough, the bees fill the cells in the beehive and eventually seal the tops to keep the honey safe. Once both sides of the frame are full, the beekeeper can harvest the honey.

To get the honey, the farmer puts the frame in a spinner. As it spins, the honey comes off the frame and settles into the bottom of the spinner barrel. The beekeeper opens the tap at the bottom of the spinner barrel, and the honey comes out. When finished straining, it's time to put the honey into jars so that it can be sent to the grocery store. Let's thank a farmer so that kids like you can enjoy sweet honey on your toast."

"See how many different farmers are out there growing the food that we get to buy in our grocery store? This is only a handful of the farms out there. Thank you to all the hardworking farmers for growing the food in our fridges and on our tables so that we can make yummy, healthy meals for our families."

End

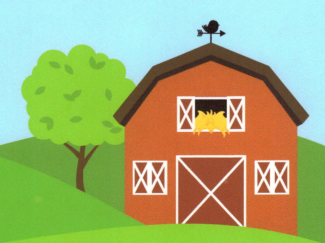

About the Author

Andrea got inspired to write **Thank a Farmer** after realizing just how many children believe that their food comes from the back room of grocery stores. Andrea wants to help teach children about the different places that food comes from and how much hard work is put into feeding the world. Andrea is a fifth-generation farmer. She farms next to her dad in Michigan and hopes that their family farm will go on for generations to come.

CPSIA information can be obtained
at www.ICGtesting.com
Printed in the USA
LVHW011050230623
750608LV00036B/247